Stylists Are Business Owners Too

DEDICATION

I dedicate this book to my friends and family for all their encouragement, love and support throughout the years.

ISBN-13: 978-1940128146
ISBN-10: 1940128145

ACKNOWLEDGEMENTS

I would like to acknowledge Mimi McCarthy for all her contributions in writing this book, Emmy Intoppa for all the research and efforts put into creating this book, and Richard W. Huntley Jr. for the endless hours put into editing this book to make it a success.

STYLISTS ARE BUSINESS OWNERS TOO!

STYLISTS ARE BUSINESS OWNERS TOO

SECTION ONE

YOUR CHAIR IS YOUR BUSINESS!

Welcome to" Stylists are Business Owners Too!" Stylists often fail when they do not think of their chair and styling station as their own. In this segment I will review the importance of treating your styling station as if it were your own business.

In section one, I will teach you the tricks and techniques to be successful behind the chair and will go over the importance of image, outstanding customer service, cleanliness, and being updated technically on all the newest trends.

In this section, although it is titled "for new stylists," I offer a step-by-step guide for any salon professional on how to find the right salon that would be a great fit for you. Although this workshop is geared for stylists, there is a place for the owner too, as I offer suggestions to help the salon owner help their stylists achieve their best. I so enjoy sharing this information with you, so let's get started!

Perhaps you've just graduated cosmetology school and you're ready to hit the floor, or you just moved across the country and you don't know a soul, or you are presently at a salon where you need to build a more solid customer base, or you have chosen to be a booth renter. Whatever the reasons you have for needing to make it a top priority to build your clientele, this workshop will help you to become the best entrepreneur ever.

Before you start to market for clients, define what type of client you want in your chair. Take some time. Write down a description of your ideal client. Include age, taste in hairstyles and lifestyles as part of your description. The more detailed your description, the easier it will be for you to determine how to build your clientele:

Once you have written goals on the type of client you will target, then if you are not currently at a salon, you will need to determine the type of salon and atmosphere in which you wish to work.

I always encourage a stylist who is looking for a salon to go in first as a customer to get a feel for the place. Think like a client. Is the customer service great, are the stylists dressed professionally, and is it a place in which you would be proud to work? Choose a location that will provide built-in ways to get new clients. For example, a mall is a great place to work if you are new to the area because it has a lot of traffic. Ask, and make sure, a salon is actively pre-booking appointments, offers on-going education, and has a hands-on owner or manager who believes in doing promotions on a monthly basis. This indicates the shop cares about bringing in new clients - and retaining them. I go into this job search process in more detail in chapter three.

But for now, let's assume you are working in a salon and have been successful in building a clientele. Now you must keep those clients coming back to YOU. You are competing not only with outside salon businesses, but you are also competing with stylists within your salon.

This is why it is so important to differentiate yourself from the rest of the staff. In doing this, though, you must remember to always maintain a team-member mentality.

So the first step is to take the time to go over some very important questions that I would like you to answer carefully. You will use this questionnaire to re-evaluate your business and get it on the right track.

- Is your chair making you money? Yes__ No__ If not, you need to look at all the ideas we go over in this workshop and re-evaluate your business.

- Is your station clean and orderly? Yes__ No__ No one wants to sit in clutter and have you use dirty tools.

- Are you pampering, pampering, and pampering your clients? Yes__ No___ If you are not, someone else will. A client will continue to return to a place where she is made to feel good inside and out.

- Do you have impeccable customer service skills? Yes___No__ Poor guest service is a main reason why a client will not return. If you are not making your client feel like she is the most valuable being alive, someone else will.

- Are you up to date on all the newest trends and technical skills? Yes___ No__ On-going education is critical for all stylists in order to stay on top of their game. Keeping updated allows you to be able to introduce new and trendy styles to your clients. It is so important that you know how to duplicate a specific style when your client wants her hair to look like her favorite celebrity.

- Are you always professionally dressed, with make-up applied, and your hair styled fashionably? Yes___ No__ You can't expect to sell fashion and beauty to your client if you are not sporting it yourself. A client will be attracted to the stylist who is dressed professionally, with clean, styled hair and tastefully applied makeup.

- Are you prepared for your clients? Do you offer on-time service? Yes_____ No_____ We all run behind schedule at one time or another. Clients really appreciate it when they are not made to wait for their appointments. However, if you happen to run late, make sure your client is comfortable waiting with something to drink and read.

- Ask yourself, would you want to sit in your chair if you were the client? Yes____No__ Always look at your station through the eyes of a customer. Make sure your station is clean and orderly for each client no matter how busy you get. No one wants to sit down in a chair with hair in it and look down to see hair all over the floor. Your combs and brushes should be cleaned and disinfected after each use.

- Are you dependable and flexible with your clients? Yes___No___ When I was working behind the chair, I made it a point to stay late or come in early for my clients when it was necessary. This is especially important when building a loyal clientele. I always tried to accommodate the client that had an unexpected dinner or other engagement to go to and needed me to squeeze her in to do her hair for the event. It's just good business.

- Do you show passion and enthusiasm for your work? Yes___No___ There is nothing worse than to have a stylist who seems bored and who doesn't seem to want to be at work. I tell stylists they must treat their profession like a career and not like a dull job they go to each day to collect a pay check. Your clients will be able to tell, and they won't come back to you. If you are feeling in a rut, try talking to someone you feel comfortable with (perhaps your salon owner or manager), and ask for suggestions. You might consider taking a motivational class to tap into your passion again. And always, always invest in on-going education. It helps to keep you motivated and will give you fresh ideas to offer your clients.

- Are your delivering the highest quality and predictable results to your customers? Yes__ No__Pampering your clients and offering exceptional customer service are crucial when building a loyal clientele, but so is delivering outstanding end results. You must be able to address your client's hair needs accurately and give her a style that is most suitable for her.

- So keep yourself updated on the newest trends and keep yourself technically trained on all haircuts and chemical services.

- Again, I bring this up because it is important:

- Is your position as a stylist your career or just a job? Career_____Job _____

It is so important for stylists to view their position as a career where they have chosen a specific path, have received the proper training, and are then willing to keep updated all the time.

Make sure you have gone through all of these questions and have answered them thoroughly one by one. Be honest when answering and be ready to change the things that will put you on top of your game.

Please utilize the "Setting Goals Action Plan" and "Profit and Loss" worksheets provided in this section to help you set goals that will help to increase your total service and retail sales.

PROFIT AND LOSS STATEMENT FOR STYLISTS
Monthly Expenses

Expenses	JAN	FEB	MAR	APR	MAY	JUNE	JULY	AUG	SEPT	OCT	NOV	DEC
Chair Rental												
Promotions												
Advertising												
Credit Card Fee												
Product Cost												
Retail Costs												
insurance												
Operating Cost												
Miscellaneous												
License Fee												
Education												
Cell Phone												
Uniform/Clothing												
TOTAL MONTHLY EXPENSES												

Monthly Sales

Sales	JAN	FEB	MAR	APR	MAY	JUNE	JULY	AUG	SEPT	OCT	NOV	DEC
Service Sales												
Retail Sales												
TOTAL MONTHLY SALES												

Calculate Your Profit/Loss

	JAN	FEB	MAR	APR	MAY	JUNE	JULY	AUG	SEPT	OCT	NOV	DEC
Total Monthly Sales												
Total Monthly Expenses												
PROFIT/LOSS:												

Stylist Worksheet – Strengths and Weaknesses

Stylist: Date:

Busiest Hours		Slowest Hours	
Busiest Days		Slowest Days	
Most Popular Services	1 2 3	Least Popular Services	1 2 3
Your Technical Strengths	1 2 3	Your Technical Weaknesses	1 2 3
$ Amount of Retail per Month	$	$ Amount of Up-Selling per Month	$

Question	Always	Sometimes	Never
Do you provide good customer service?			
Do you up-sell services?			
Do you sell retail?			
Do you experience walk-out clients?			
Do you ever have to re-do services?			
Do you set up weekly/monthly goals?			
Do you have a professional appearance?			
Is your station always ready for the next client?			
Is your station clean and organized?			

Make your "Dream/wish List!:"

1

2

3

4

Make a list of areas that need changing and improving.

1

2

3

4

Setting Goals Action Plan

SERVICES	PRICE	TOTAL # DONE	TOTAL $	NEW GOAL #	FORECASTED $ INCREASE	New Total
Women's Haircut and Finish						
Color Services						
Highlight Services						
Multi-Dimensional						
Glossing						
5-7 Foils						
Blow Dries						
Kid's Cuts						
Men's Cuts						
Texturizing (Perming)						
Straightening						
Accessorizing The Hair						
Deep Protein Treatments						
Moisturizing Treatments						
Waxing						
Facials						
Teeth Whitening						

You will find specific business building suggestions to help you create your action plan throughout the book.

Now let us continue to probe a little deeper and see how you perceive yourself.

I am a FIRM believer that we eventually become what we think. Negative thinking will affect the way you view yourself and others. I have lived by the statement, whatever comes after the thought or words "I am

_____ "

is exactly what you will become. For example, if you tell yourself, "I am talented," then the chances are, you will be talented! But on the other hand if you tell yourself, "I am uncreative then chances are you will not even try tasks that you feel may require creativity.

Negative thinking emits negative energy. A client can feel when there is friction with staff and when the salon has negative energy. I have witnessed situations where clients would not go back to a salon for the sole reason that they felt so uncomfortable with the way the staff treated each other.

So remind yourself that the mind is like a garden. You will need to weed out all the negative and polluted thinking and replace it with positive affirming thoughts. Otherwise the weeds will choke out all the beautiful things that could grow.

You also have to remember that you cannot control anyone else's behavior but your own. Don't get caught up in senseless gossip or fall into the negative trap. And most importantly, leave your personal problems at the door when you arrive at wor To be a complete success, you can't just rely on your boss. Self-promotion is so important whether you are the new kid on the block or have been working in the salon for years. I made it a practice to hand out my business card to everyone I met - in restaurants, night clubs, grocery stores, etc. I used to volunteer to work at fashion and bridal shows, and I used to do makeovers for local news anchors in order to get noticed.

Once you have established a growing customer base, start asking for their help in bringing you their friends and family.

Let them know you are looking for new customers and promise to reward them if they help you.

A method that always worked for me was referral cards. Give each client three to five of your business cards and have your client put his or her name on the back. When all of those cards have come back to the salon in the hands of new clients, give your original customer a free service or product.

Let's talk more about having a Successful Referral Program.

You can either use your business cards as I described above, or you can order preprinted referral cards. If you use the preprinted referral cards, here is how I suggest you do it:

1. At the end of every service, give each of your client's three referral cards. Explain to them that when they refer a friend who brings in the referral card, the new client and the existing client will both receive a special gift. Tell them to be sure to fill out the card with their name and address and to do the same for the person they are referring.

2. Each time a new client comes in with a referral card, present her with the gift of your choice—a free product, an add-on service, a discount, etc. You can fill in the blank with your choice of gift.

3. I always mailed a gift certificate to clients who referred their friends to me to use toward their next service. Don't forget to make the certificate valid for a specific period of time, such as 30 days. This will encourage clients to book their next appointment right away in order to use their gift certificate, before it expires, and get their discount.

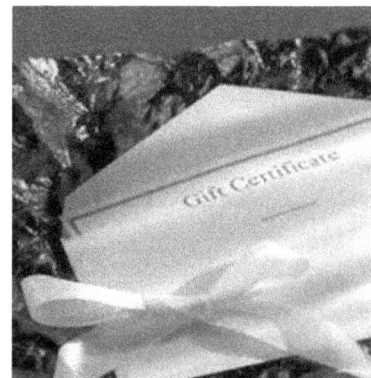

It doesn't take a rocket scientist to know that clients are stretching out the time between appointments. But what you may be surprised to learn is how much money you're losing when clients don't return every six weeks. In a down economy, pre-booking is a sure winner.

I had huge success getting my clients to pre-book early, and I will share with you how I did that.

First, you will need to determine the gift you will be providing to clients when they pre-book their next appointment. Make sure it is a gift that will build your business, such as a retail product, a complimentary add-on service, or dollars off their next service.

Consider changing it up every few months.

Next, you, the stylist, should make out your own cards with your name and the reward you have decided to give that client. Then, make sure to place your pre-book cards on your station where they are visible. You may even want to put up a cute card on your mirror saying, "Ask me how you can save money on your next appointment." If you forget to mention the cards, the client will most likely ask how.

Remember, you want to reward your clients for getting back into your chair before they even leave it.

Consider using punch cards too. They are a great way to get clients back into your chair. Punch cards are catching on in many retail businesses. And why not? Everyone is looking for deals, so why not reward your clients for coming to see you for services and for buying their retail in your salon.

In my salons I created two different punch cards, one for services and one for retail products.

Here is how you do it:

1. First, establish the value of each punch hole.
2. Next, establish the value of a fully punched card. For example, will you offer a free service or free retail product once the card is fully punched?
3. Place the cards in acrylic holders at your station.
4. After a service or retail purchase, fill in the client's name, the value for each punch, the award for a completed punch card, and the expiration date. Present a completed card to every client.
5. Once services are rendered or retail is purchased, punch the card for your client.
6. Each time your client returns, ask for her punch card. Don't count on the receptionist to do this for you.
7. Once the card is filled, with punches, award the gift for a completed card.

Okay, so what happens if you can't afford to get these different cards? Why not try teaming up with other stylists and splitting the costs? Obviously, it will be more cost efficient than getting them printed yourself. This will also generate excitement amongst the staff.

So stylists, find a way to utilize these various card programs. Your customers will feel appreciated and rewarded which, in turn, will entice them to become the town crier on your behalf!

Next, we want to probe a little bit deeper with a few more questions. Write down as much information as you can so that you will be able to build a realistic plan going forward.

Describe your present situation. For example, what types of money are you making? How strong is your customer base? Is your retention of clients good, or is it the best?

Now write down where you want to be. For example, I want to be making x amount of money so I can purchase a car, a house, etc.

Next, jot down the changes you would like to implement in your business. Keep in mind that once you put all this information together, you should plan to start by doing it one change at a time. No need to overwhelm yourself. The first mile of a journey is taken with the first step.

Now, armed with all of the information you have gathered in these pages of questions we have covered, it is time to create an action plan and to put a strategy in place to strengthen the areas that need improvement.

So write an action plan stating how you can be more successful in building and re- tailing a solid clientele. Here are some examples. I need to keep my styling station cleaner. I need to take some motivational classes so I feel more inspired in my job.

I need to be more proactive in taking control of my business in order to grow my customer base.

.

My action plan will be:

_____

_____

_____

_____

_____

_____

_____

_____

_____

_____

You will find specific business building suggestions throughout the rest of the work- book.

Now let's continue to probe a little deeper and see how you perceive yourself.

I am a firm believer that we eventually become what we think. Negative thinking will affect the way you view yourself and others. I have lived by the statement, whatever comes after the thought or words "I am" is exactly what you will become. For ex- ample, if you tell yourself, "I am talented," then the chances are, you will be talented! But on the other hand if you tell yourself, "I am uncreative," then the chances are you won't even try tasks that you feel require creativity.

Negative thinking emits negative energy. A client can feel when there is friction with staff and when the salon has negative energy. I have witnessed situations where clients would not go back to a salon for the sole reason that they felt so uncomfortable with the way the staff treated each other.

So remind yourself that the mind is like a garden. You need to weed out all the negative and polluted thinking and replace it with positive affirming thoughts. Otherwise the weeds will choke out all the beautiful things that could grow.

You also have to remember that you cannot control anyone else's behavior but your own. Do not get caught up in senseless gossip or fall into the negative trap. Most importantly, leave your personal problems at the door when you arrive at work.

To be a complete success, you can't just rely on your boss. Self -promotion is so important whether you are the new kid on the block or have been working in the salon for years. I made it a practice to hand out my business card to everyone I met - in restaurants, night clubs, grocery stores, etc. I used to volunteer to work at fashion and bridal shows, and I used to do makeovers for local news anchors in order to get noticed.

Once you have established a growing customer base, start asking for their help in bringing you their friends and family.

Let them know you are looking for new customers and promise to reward them if they help you.

A method that always worked for me was referral cards. Give each client three to five of your business cards and have your client put his or her name on the back. When all of those cards have come back to the salon in the hands of new clients, give your original customer a free service or product.

Let's talk more about having a Successful Referral Program.

You can either use your business cards as I described above, or you can order pre- printed referral cards. If you use the preprinted referral cards, here is how I suggest you do it:

1. Fill in the referral cards with the salon's name and your name and information. Place these cards in a clear acrylic holder at YOUR station.

2. At the end of every service, give each of your clients' three referral cards. Ex- plain to them that when they refer a friend who brings in the referral card, the new client and the existing client will both receive a special gift. Tell them to be sure to fill out the card with their name and address and to do the same for the person they are referring.

3. Each time a new client comes in with a referral card, present her with the gift of your choice—a free product, an add-on service, a discount, etc. You can fill in the blank with your choice of gift.

4. I always mailed a gift certificate postcard to clients who referred their friends to me to use toward their next service. Don't forget to make the certificate valid for a specific period of time, such as 30 days. This will encourage clients to book their next appointment right away in order to use their gift certificate postcard, before it expires, and get their discount.

It doesn't take a rocket scientist to know that clients are stretching out the time between appointments. But what you may be surprised to learn is how much money you're losing when clients don't return every six weeks. In a down economy, pre-booking is a sure winner.

I had huge success getting my clients to pre-book early, and I will share with you how I did that.

First, you will need to determine the gift you will be providing to clients when they pre-book their next appointment. Make sure it's a gift that will build your business, such as a retail product, a complimentary add-on service, or dollars off their next service.

Consider changing it up every few months.

Next, you, the stylist, should make out your own cards with your name and the re- ward you have decided to give that client. Then, make sure to place your pre-book cards on your station where they are visible. You may even want to put up a cute card on your mirror saying, "Ask me how you can save money on your next appointment." If you forget to mention the cards, the client will most likely ask how.

Remember, you want to reward your clients for getting back into your chair before they even leave it.

Consider using punch cards too. They are a great way to get clients back into your chair. Punch cards are catching on in many retail businesses, and why not? Everyone is looking for deals, so why not reward your clients for coming to see you for services and for buying their retail in your salon. In my salons I created two different punch cards, one for services and one for retail products.

1. First, establish the value of each punch hole.

2. Next, establish the value of a fully punched card. For example, will you offer a free service or free retail product once the card is fully punched?

3. Place the cards in acrylic holders at your station.

4. After a service or retail purchase, fill in the client' s name, the value for each punch, the award for a completed punch card, and the expiration date. Present a completed card to e v e r y client.

5. Once services are rendered or retail is purchased, punch the card for your client.

6. Each time your client returns, ask for her punch card. Don' t count on the receptionist to do this for you. Once the card is filled with punches, award the gift for a completed card.

7. Okay, so what happens if you can' t afford to get these different cards? Why not try teaming up with other stylists and splitting the costs? Obviously, it will be more cost efficient than getting them printed yourself. This will also generate excitement amongst the staff.

8. So stylists, find a way to utilize these various card programs. Your customers will feel appreciated and rewarded which, in turn, will entice them to become the town crier on your behalf!

STYLISTS ARE BUSINESS OWNERS TOO

SECTION TWO

A SPECIAL NOTE FOR NEW STYLISTS

So you have made it through school with flying colors, and now you are ready to hit the real world!

In this section, I will offer some suggestions to help you find the right job for you, and I will help you prepare to be a huge success. Get ready to put together a simple business plan that will assist you in getting organized and help you find a salon that will be a nice fit for you.

Although this guide has been written with new graduates in mind, the information I offer is beneficial for any salon professional at any stage in his/her career.

My first suggestion is for you to make a list of things that you should discover about a salon that would entice you to work at that specific salon. The best way to do this is to visit the salons that you are interested in applying to as a customer, first, before you schedule an interview. As a customer, how do you feel about the salon and the staff? For example, do the stylists get along, and do they work together well as a team? Is the customer service impeccable? Are the stylists and front desk staff friendly and accommodating? Is the salon clean and inviting? Is the atmosphere friendly, and does the salon exude warmth? Are the technical skills of the stylists who are doing hair current and up-to-date? Another question you should ask yourself is do you want to work in a full-service salon or a salon that offers just haircuts and styles?

List the things that are important to you in a salon in which you would consider working:

_____

_____

_____

_____

I suggest that brand new, graduating stylists not apply at high- end salons and end up working as an assistant. So many times I have seen stylists lose their technical skills because they are doing only shampoos and occasional blow-dries. Clients tend to label these new stylists as assistants and don't always give them the chance to be a stylist for them. Instead,

I would suggest starting at a chain salon that offers full training and on- going education and that also does lots of advertising to help stylists to build their clientele.

So now you have narrowed down your list to salons that you would love to work in, and you have set up an interview with the manager and owner, but first, you must make another plan. Incentive programs are important because incentives allow the stylist to stay motivated, they create excitement in the salon with the clients and staff, and they provide a great way to earn extra money. Stylists are more apt to remain at a salon where they are motivated, happy, and earning extra money!

- What does the owner expect of his/her employees? It is so important that you know what the owner's expectations are and what your job description will be.

- For example, does the owner require you to retail a certain percentage of sales each week, and does the owner require a certain production per hour for your service sales? It benefits both the stylist and the owner to have a clear understanding of the owner's expectations so that the stylist can determine if he/she is comfortable with those expectations.

- What types of benefits does the salon offer? For example, health insurance, paid holidays, paid ongoing educational classes, etc.

- What are the work shifts like? If you have limitations on when you can work this has to be addressed upfront in the interview.

- What types of goals are set for you by the salon? For example, are you expected to retail, and if so, is there a separate commission for retail?

The ideal situation is where the salon offers an additional commission for retail above and beyond your regular pay.

- Is there an orientation period to help you transition into your first real job? Ideally you should be offered a period of orientation because it will help you to familiarize yourself with the salon and the staff. I used to have a buddy system where my new stylist would work closely with my manager or a senior stylist for about one month. At that point, most new stylists were comfortable with their surroundings and knew where to find all the tools and supplies necessary for work, so they are comfortable enough to do just fine on their own.

List the items you want to discuss during a salon interview:

_____

_____

_____

Remember that the more information you find out about a salon, the staff, and their policies ahead of time, the more likely you are to find a salon that is a good fit for you. Also, remember that hopping from salon to salon is not good for your career. So, do your homework ahead of time, and note that it takes time (a good year anyway) to build a clientele. So be prepared to stay at the salon you chose and give it a chance!

It is always so exciting to begin a new opportunity. Enjoy this time, make it count for all it's worth, and I wish you success!

ABOUT THE AUTHOR

Jeanne Degen is a leader in the beauty industry. For 33 years, she has brought her expertise to salons, manufacturers and distributorships as an educator, a trainer, a stylist and as a successful salon owner. Now she has created Positive Salon Strategies, a salon consulting company that delivers easily accessible, proven business strategies to salon professionals in the beauty profession.

Her 10-minute online workshops are designed as easy to follow, step-by- step instructional programs that allow salon professionals to learn effective techniques for business success. The workshops feature tips and strategies that Jeanne herself used to manage and grow her salon business. She knows how hectic running a salon can be, and she is confident and excited that the short format instruction provided by Positive Salon Strategies will help others to be more successful at operating their businesses.

Jeanne brings impressive professional experience to bear in her company. As Director of Operations and Education at Fantastic Sam' s International Corp, she has assisted franchisees nationwide to build salon revenue. She not only offered education and operational support to established salons, but also supervised and conducted new salon opening trainings, including interviewing and hiring new staff. She has taught and created workshops that address employee turnover, that motivate staff to sell, create winning salon promotions, power re- tailing, and that help create great customer service, among many other topics. Jeanne also consulted with salon owners and franchisees on profitability, inventory control, client retention, and all business aspects necessary for operating a successful salon.

Jeanne has also held positions at internationally acclaimed companies, including various beauty Distributors, National Director of Education at ISO and National Education and Sales Manager at Helene Curtis. She has hands-on stylist experience and has performed platform work with some of the most elite platform artists in the industry. Most importantly, Jeanne is thrilled to realize her dream of supporting the growth and prosperity of the salon community through her company, Positive Salon Strategies.